And This is What Happens Next

Books Published by Marcus Rome

Abreactions, Birch Brook Press, 1989

Visual Eyes, Ziggurat Press, 1997

Repercussions, Birch Brook Press, 2000

Out of Darkness, St. Bede's Publications, 2000

Confessions of a Rational Lunatic, Birch Brook Press, 2006

And This is What Happens Next, Birch Brook Press, 2010

MARCUS ROME

And This is What Happens Next

BIRCH BROOK PRESS

Copyright © 2010 by Marcus Rome

All rights reserved. Except for brief passages in a review or interview, no part of this book may be reproduced in any form, by any means, without permission in writing from the publisher.

First Edition

ISBN: 978-0-9789974-9-6

Library of Congress Control No.: 2009909549

Art by: Bertha Rogers

Published by:

>   Birch Brook Press
>   PO Box 81
>   Delhi, NY 13753

For more information about this book and other titles published by this and other authors, please visit our website:

>   www.birchbrookpress.info

birchbrook@copper.net

CONTENTS

The Last Word/9
Land of the Prophets/11
Relativity/12
A Trace of Doubt/13
Safe House/14
Posted: No Trespassing/15
Interrogation/17
Side Show/19
Hearsay/22
The Dealer to the Table/23
It's an Inside Job/25
Mr. Peter van den Heuvel &
    The Law of Diminishing Returns/27
$99.95 Happiness/28
Bon Appetit/30
American Carminative/32
Twentieth Century Fox Presents/33
The Poets Are All Insane/36
The Social Register/39
The Man Who Became a Period/40
The Appropriate Man/41
Jake/42
Professor/43
Omniscient Narrator/44
The Meticulous Man/46
Coffee/48
My Favorite White Tail Tall Tale/49
Harvest Time/51

Sunday Visits/52
The Secret/53
Hamlet in the Afternoon/54
Loss of Innocence/56
It's All Good/57
Zen and Aunt Ida's Alphabet Soup/59
Falling from Your Mind/61
M.I.A./63
The Timeless Man/64
The Man Who Went Too Far/65
The Man Who Waited
    For the Sky to Fall/66
Forget About It/67
Do Over/68
So What Took You So Long?/70

ABOUT THE AUTHOR/71
ABOUT THE BOOK/72

for Andrea

The Last Word

The clock runs backwards
until time runs out
until the sun holds still
and the shadows disappear
and the song birds go mute
and you become deaf
to the words and the books
ever spoken by man
of woman not born
while the mustard seed roots down in the valley
and spreads through the land
of brother with brother sharing the plow
of sister and sister sharing a bed
with the sons and daughters of men like you
where the mustard seed takes root in the womb
and spreads forgiveness through the land of your fathers
all covered in blood where time becomes time
until it runs out
and you become you of the mustard seed born
who hears the song borne in the wind
of a warm gentle breath that blows in your ear
like the mustard seed coming to rest
to become the you you never had in your mind
of the son of man of a woman born
that slaughtered your sister and mother and brother
to become more than the mustard seed ever had in mind
and you stand still in time your hands dripping with the blood
of the sons and daughters you used in your war
to have the last word ever spoken or written
to fall in the ear of your sons not born

where no shadows ever fall
and the sun stands still
and the birds never sing
and the wind never blows before dawn.

Land of the Prophets

One man is killed for
whatever
one man kills for
whatever
another reads the Dead Sea scroll for
whatever
and preaches what he reads
on the salty waters that divide the land
of how brothers kill brothers
who covet their sisters and their mothers
and lie in wait for their fathers to sleep
of fathers grown gray who covet their daughters
and remind their sons while still in the cradle
who holds the blade against all of their dreams
in all the land of milk and honey and unleavened bread
where mothers give birth and organize the day
while boys are out just being boys
and prophets are out walking on water
prophesying about tomorrow and yesterday.

You at home listen for anything out of the ordinary
that would change tomorrow or yesterday for today
in this land of whatever and anon
where women bury sons
and organize the day for tomorrow
before the prophets have anything to say about it.

Relativity

The second becomes
the minute becomes
the hour becomes
the day becomes
the week becomes
the month becomes
the year becomes
time present becomes
time past has no beginning
time to be no end.

We invent instruments
for measuring the immeasurable
timelessness of time.
To keep our minds from falling off the edge
we insist on the correct time at all times
and a calendar to mark our birthday.

There are no instruments to count the dead,
to measure the pain of the weeping mothers left behind
or weigh the invisible idea of the martyrs.

Time present is a gap
in the continuity of consciousness.
The long-term vision sustains us
through the short-term disappointments.
The forward movement of the species is inevitable
as the idea feeds itself to death
and we give birth to tomorrow.

A Trace of Doubt

While reading your book
you notice a fallen hair
caught in the spine
between page 129 and page 130
at the end of chapter 20
and the start of chapter 21
"The Necessity of War"
"The Cost of War"

Someone not you
scratched his head

You know the need and the price
you're an American
you're a capitalist
you believe in God
country and family
the innocence of children
and we need to know
who read this book last and had doubts
we need to keep better records
at the library

Chapter 22
"The Spoils of War"

Safe House

Sometimes out of the corner of my eye
I catch the movement of a figure in the room
a reflection in the window
a passing cloud a falling leaf the wind
will do to keep my mind
from spilling over into something deep
inside me that feels watched
by a hidden spectator passing judgment
on my mind
on all the thoughts words and deeds
that have ever been or are about to be
the measure of myself as I am
will do to keep my eyes diverted
from the reflecting pool
where I baptize innocents
into this world of our doing
every Sunday afternoon
when we divert our reflection
from everything we are
to everything we could be
in the tabernacle of our collective selves
where no one is left to wither on the vine
and we can all walk naked in our own house
safe and with nothing to hide
from the hidden spectator of our reflection

Posted: No Trespassing

You do not give your name
you say no word
without me
I am your mouthpiece
I will do your talking
before you give it away
whether you mean to or not
in what you say and how you look
whisper
it in my ear
how it went down
I will prove your innocence
to the man
at the table of twelve
whisper
you cannot be trusted
whisper
you will give it away
before I can prove your innocence.

We are all damaged but we get used to it
if you listen to yourself
like in your dream
you will hear yourself
behind the word
to what you mean
to where you give yourself away
to where you want to look away
to where you see yourself
in a two-way mirror
looking in on yourself
and everything you have to say

giving everything away
you never had in mind
it is just that way
all along the way
to finish where you started.

It is all free if you listen
to yourself thinking
behind the mirror
to what you think you hear
coming from the reflection
you never heard before
now that you have the rhythm down
the words flow
to forgive you
for anything you had in mind
someplace deep down in your dream
where you are innocent
just like me
and I am as clean as new fallen snow
glistening under the new moon.

We are all damaged but we get used to it
that is what I am here for
to see you through
the other side of yourself
to where you forgive those
who forgive you
for being without a mind to
just as it was in your dream
beyond the weathered trespass sign
where you gather the damaged
deep in your arms and forgive them
for not knowing what they did
in your dream last night.

Interrogation

Lately
my movements are measured.
I'm suspicious of myself.
Have I broken any laws today?
Ignorance I'm told is no excuse.
Santa really knows now
if you've been naughty or good,
he has devices now
that look and listen
everywhere all the time now.
Can I hold up to an interrogation?
How long will it take?
How much can I take
before I tell you
what you want to hear?

Yesterday
in the park
while sitting on a slatted bench
my stare wandered
through the spaces
between the iron bars
into the playground
to the amber mother
pushing the ivory child
floating in the arching swing,
skirts billowing in the innocent wind.

My mind wandered.
And now you want to know where
I wandered to in the absence.

What is it you want to hear
me confess to?
What do you have in mind?
If you tell me
I can help you
hear what you want to hear
from me that you already
have in mind
but won't confess to.
If you help me
I'll help you
get your confession
from me.

So how about it,
come clean with me
so I can help you
get it off your chest
once and for all
so you can go to heaven
in the end,
clean as new fallen Christmas snow.

Side Show

Come this way
step a little closer
that's right folks
gather round listen up
and I'll tell you what I'm gonna do
for two bits a quarter of a dollar
two thin dimes and a nickle
are all it takes to get you into
this wondrous wonderland of wonderment
where all the secrets of the ages
are revealed to you
one and all
that's right
thank you
watch your step please
go right in.

Gather round the crystal sphere
that fills the center of the tent
and as the fog begins to clear
embrace its age old wisdom
as the sand embraces rain
begin to understand
why today never ends
tomorrow is a dream
and knowledge is but yesterday
as the fog begins to clear
and the never ending stranger
begins now to appear
to tell you all the truth
that two bits will procure

and reveal the reason you're all here
around this crystal sphere
searching for the truth
as you stare into the sphere
learn to be invisible
in plain view
to the never ending stranger
as you look deep into the sphere
where two bits brought you
and curiosity keeps you
looking for the meaning
of a memory you never had.

Step a little closer
that's right folks
avert your eyes from everything
but the crystal sphere
cast your eyes upon
the never ending stranger
that now appears
through the dissipating fog
watch as he dismembers time
before your very eyes
so that all that ever was is
and all that will be is
here before you now
as I pass the basket around
drop in your watches and your coin
show your neighbor
you believe in Him
who stands outside time
as you believe in yourself
and splendiferous eternity.

Step a little quicker
that's right folks
backwards to the door
and take with you a memory
you never had before
and all this
imagine that
for two bits
and a little of your time.

Hearsay

I've heard from reliable sources
that the meek, poor and powerless
shall inherit everlasting happiness
while the rich and powerful
will surely burn in hell
for their avarice.
This thought lightly floats
across my mind
from a far-off voice
as I wait my turn
on the lottery ticket line
but I conclude this an ideal
time to keep my mouth shut
and take my chances
along with everyone else
that there will be enough
time at the end
for an act of contrition.

The Dealer to the Table

If you never get used to it
you never miss it
says the dealer to the table
I keep you straight
with no addictions
independent and on your own
just like you first came in
I deal you everything but hearts
to keep your mind from wandering
to something you can't have
without paying for it
you came in here to give it up
not to take it home

You keep your house hushed like
a well-polished church
you eat take out and go to bed early
you sip hot coffee from a paper cup
while lovers row on the lake
you watch a golden leaf
drop in the autumn breeze

You're here to be a rascal
your hand wrapped tight around your wad
feels warm to the touch
as you take in the life in the room
and everything you can have for a price
like the pretty lady playing roulette
that smiles your way
you're here to give it up
not to take anything home
that wants to change the arrangement

The dealer knows the other side of you
like the card he's about to turn
he knows you're here to give it up
not to take it home
he makes sure you never get addicted
dependent or take it home
he never deals you a queen of hearts
over an ace of spades
and never asks a question
you have no answer to
you rascal you

It's an Inside Job

It's an inside job
all agreed at the scene
no forcible entry
no picked lock
no glass on the floor.

Someone had to know
the time of day
and when the safe was full.

There are no fingerprints to be had
no DNA
just the scent of warm cinnamon buns on Sunday morning.

It had to be an inside job
someone knew the tumblers
someone knew the time
someone knew what the job paid
someone had it in his mind that crime pays
someone had his bent brittle father on his mind
someone had it in his mind that he could get away
pulling what he pulled in church that day
thinking he could escape
the scent of warm cinnamon buns
on Sunday mornings.

It must have been an inside job
all the clues point that way
all we gotta do is examine the possibilities:
I was eating cinnamon buns watching TV
doing everything I wanted to
holy as could be.

It must have been an inside job
no one outside knows the time
when the sun goes down or the moon comes up
the clock has one hand the blinds are down
it must have been an inside job.

No clues at the scene of the crime
and I'm the only one in town without an alibi.
Has anyone ever seen me eating cinnamon buns
or know where to find me Sunday mornings?

It must have been an inside job
given what we know
and the time of day.
I got nothing more to say
given the time of day
that ain't already been on your mind
that you're itching for me to say.

I was in church Sunday morning
while you were home watching TV
wishing you could be me.

Everybody's convinced
it was an inside job
and the finger always points to me
while the sweet smell of cinnamon fills the air
and points to you.

Mr. Peter van den Heuvel &
The Law of Diminishing Returns

Mr. Peter van den Heuvel was weaned on
the law of diminishing returns
which states that effort and hard work
pay off up to the point that
they don't anymore
do what they used to do.

And so Mr. Peter van den Heuvel asks himself
if this is the law and I'm no law breaker
and I've paid my dues
served my country
done right by the kids
been faithful to the wife
played by the rules of honest hard work
yet the returns keep diminishing
year in and year out
no matter the effort no matter the time
and the fat corporate cat
licks the cream from his chops
with the weary price of work
furrowed deep in my brow
I quietly ask with a clear conscience
isn't it fine
isn't it time
isn't it reasonable
for us to stop now
since we're all just so bushed from running in place.

Even the weariest river
winds its way somewhere safe to sea
sure to be reborn as the gem of the ocean.

$99.95 Happiness

If I had one
I'd be happy
the man on TV
said to me
he told me
to call today
right now
and see for myself
how happy I could be
for $99.95
satisfaction guaranteed

Sounded good to me
so I bought what he said
for $99.95
plugged it in
sat still
and breathed deeply
just like the instructions said
for 40 days and 40 nights
I didn't leave the house
and I didn't get happy
I just got mad
that I'd been had

I couldn't take no more
and so I called
the man on TV
and told him
I was real mad
that I'd been had
and wanted him

to send me
my $99.95
back to me
right away

He told me
he was only
a TV actor
that read a script
to pay the rent
and buy the baby new shoes
he said
I needed to talk
to the Big Man
for that
but when I called
I was told
the Big Man
only spoke to happy people

I knew there
was only one solution

And so
I wait
in the alley shadows
of the Big Man's office
breathing deeply
in and out
waiting patiently
to collect
my $99.95
worth of satisfaction
and happiness guaranteed

Bon Appetit

The swells dine at the place to be
seen if you're anybody who wants to be
somebody in the morning papers.
The well-dropped complaint
that trickles from their tongue
down their upturned nose
is of necessity the sophisticated thing to do:
the wine too warm
the light too bright
the meat too tough
the water too bland
the coffee not hot enough
the service too slow and nondeferential
for the swells that hold you by the tip
of what you'll take home tonight for the wife and kids.

And in the kitchen
the brown-skinned Mexican
scrapes the plate, polishes the fork
chop, chop, chops what has to be chopped
mops the floor, scrubs the pots
and somewhere between the hours
slips into a reverie of what he's left behind:
the soft embrace of his wife
the sweet breath of his children
the daydream of the day
they join him in the U.S.A.
the daydream of the day
he has after rent enough greenbacks
enough eighteen hour minimum wage days
to buy their way into the U.S.A.
the land of opportunity and prosperity

hidden under the coffee sacks that cross the border
before the next Mexican crossing the desert comes for his job.

All this as he sits on his box
eats his dinner and stares into his mind.

All this while the swells
dip into their baked Alaska
and talk of Dow Jones.

American Carminative

I've been thinking lately since the world is running out of
stuff like air space fossil fuel and Kleenex tissues
that perhaps we should be thinking about breeding
down breeding smaller that is in stature that
is let's say to an average height of three
feet that should do to slow the
consumption rate in America
where we all take in more
than we give I'm thinking
the only way out is to
cut down to a more
reasonable size
so we fit into
smaller shoes
and take up
less than
we give
back.

You got a better idea?

Twentieth Century Fox Presents

Twentieth Century Fox
presents
The Gangster Movie
starring
Robin Hood
who took from the rich
to give to the poor
and the honorable bandits
Jesse James
Willie Sutton
and Bonnie and Clyde
who robbed banks
in the Depression just because
that's where the money was
always starring a regular guy
like you and me
born on the wrong side of the tracks
whose Pa drank himself to death
after being bled by the slaughterhouse jungle
leaving Ma to scrub the blood floors clean
to pay the rent to buy food for the nesting brood
and coal for the tin can fire
while Jimmy Cagney
the gangster's gangster
carries the pain
in the back of his neck
that only Ma's squeeze could relieve
stands tough through to the end
high atop the Jersey gas tanks
the cops in hot pursuit
look Ma I'm on top of the world Ma
and with guns blazing

he goes up
in an inferno ball of fire
taking you and me
and every other poor son of a bitch
in the darkened neighborhood
movie house
up with him
on Saturday afternoons.

And then Fox pulls the curtain down
on the honest home-grown gangster hero
and up on the imported wise guy bully
trading respect for fear
preying on the weak the ignorant
the scared hard working Joe
trying to make ends meet
in the corner candy store
being tapped for a piece of the action
by the greasy punk who knows somebody
who knows somebody only yesterday elected
until Eliot Ness pulls into town
and pulls the plug on the Chicago cowards
and the kids all cheer that the G-men are here
and Ma and Pa and Junior get saved from the scum
all on Saturday afternoons
in the neighborhood movie house.

And now
the sly Fox
draws the curtain open
on the greatest show on earth
Coca Cola, GE, Haliburton,
Big Oil, Dow Jones
and the promise

that you too can have it all
pure as snow and legit
on the backs of the have nots
who are not me and you
if you believe in God
salute the flag
and vote Republican
so why not says the old Fox
have your cake and eat it
who's the wiser for it
for the way it's always been
and Robin Hood is a long-time gone
from the silver screen
in the land of I and me
stretched across your plasma TV.

The Poets Are All Insane

The poets are all insane.
Plato knew it, Freud knew it
and now I'm telling you,
me who am a poem to be.

These guys and gals
just hang around
and pretend that they aren't
themselves or anybody at all.
They let their thoughts
take care of themselves
until they get far away
from themselves
to make a poem
about themselves.

They then expect you
who come home
from a hard day's work
to make sense
of their jibber jabber
all for yourself they say
since it's all about you they say.
Now that they've said it
they say they have nothing to do
with it anymore they say
so it's for you to get
and them not to say.

And if you don't get it
if you have to ask
if you get angry, furious or mad

well then you're just a Philistine
with no poetic soul
and no place in poetry.
Being a simple poem to be
I'm here to explain it all to you for free.

The academic critics you see
get paid very well you see
to decipher the jibber jabber for you and me.
They write books
they teach courses
to guide us through the jibber jabber
and teach the innocent MFA's
to write more jibber jabber
so they'll get tenure, raise families
and live in neat ivy cottages
while the innocent pretend
they aren't themselves
or anybody at all
but great poets
allowing their thoughts
about themselves
to take care of themselves.

While you come home
from a hard day's work
that takes care of a nation
the great poets go begging
at the critics' ivy cottage door
for yesterday's scraps
and who they used to be
as the hushed sound of dust
settles on the writing table.

You do understand now
don't you
why the poets are all insane
and I'll never be a poem.

The Social Register

A man steps on a banana peel
slips slides and thumps down his well-
padded tush. He's okay just red.
The man was delivering a cream
pie which flew from his hands as
he fell. He watched the pie come
tumbling down on the head of the good
Bishop doing a baptism spilling
the salt and holy water in the middle
of it all into the infant's eyes and
mouth who grows up thinking
she can be a poet sans Iowa
anointment of dominus vobiscum
MFA art thou amen. Let's all sit
back and have a good laugh
watching the man do the
banana peel slip.

The Man Who Became a Period

O' sure it was great fun
being a question mark
asking about this and that
full of wonder and discovery
slowly developing into a colon
listing all the things you learned and knew
then becoming a comma
as you moved into
more complex ideas
that needed more than a single breath
which compounded your dilemma
of two minds in one
when you fell upon the semicolon
to keep you in balance
and if you had a brilliant night of insight
an exclamation point would do
before the final period
and you turned off the light.

The Appropriate Man

When was it proper to applaud?
He didn't know
so he sat still
and in the end
he gave himself a hand
for perseverance
and the audience
applauded him
for standing out
in a crowd.

He loved the theater.
It was so much better
than watching TV
with his cat.

Jake

Most said it was the gin
he told me the screams
drowned out the voices
Jesus Mary Mother of God
there is nobody to take it out on
and how much can I get away with
and how do I survive
from December through April
and what do I have
to show for it all
Jake said
while his left eye delved
narrowly into the past
and his right eye gazed
wide into the future
Jesus Mary Mother of God
he found it difficult to picture
a situation that did not actually
take place in the room with him
so he shortened his thoughts
so they would not wander
out into the darkness beyond tomorrow
and far away
in the cold pale November moonlight
a man was calling someone
Jesus
most still wanted to believe
it was the gin

Professor

Prof. Mario Piccolo
the immaculately attired
bespectacled museum curator
prowls the dimly lit corridors
in soft silent cotton slippers
after hours
alone and unseen.

He gently strokes his palm
along the curves and crevices
of the smooth cool marbles.
He presses his face and lips
to the old oil canvasses and
deeply inhales the purples and reds.

He sits on the royal throne
a golden sceptre in his hand.
His head upturned and askance
he dismissively waves his arm
across the empty chamber.

He tires
and retires to his warm bed
where he dreams his special dream
of being a museum.

Omniscient Narrator

In the evening
he read his dictionary
to drown out the voices
the mindless minds
the brainless faces full of pride
promising the dream of dreams
if he only knew what he didn't know
while all he knew was what he knew
and nothing more.

He knew what side of the bed
to get up on in the morning.
He knew to always stir
his coffee from left to right
to keep the world spinning right.
To be certain about his toast
he buttered both sides.
He wore wing-tip shoes
parted his hair and
always carried an umbrella
just in case.

He knew each man
was a measure of his actions.
He knew ignorance
often mistook itself for knowledge.
He knew anatomy is destiny.
He knew all the words
of all the stories ever told.
He knew he was in none of them.
He knew we've all got it coming

we just don't know when
it's going to get here.
He knew to always carry his umbrella
just in case he found himself
in someone else's story.
He knew that if he walked
with his back to the sun
he would cast a shadow he could see.

This is all he knew
and nothing more.

In his dream of dreams
there is always sunshine
and never an umbrella.

The Meticulous Man

He was an artist with the dead.

He horded provisions
in his well-stocked pantry,
neatly stacked columns and rows
of cans and tins and jars and boxes,
always enough to keep his mind calm
just in case anyone unexpected dropped by.
He filled his bureau drawer
with light bulbs of every size
should an idea come to him in the night.
A gross of toilet paper in the closet was essential
to relieve any anal retentive residue
of an unfulfilled Oedipal conflict
that might rear its ugly head in a dream.

He had a radio and a clock in every room.

He wore spit-polished leather shoes,
creased and folded all his clothes.
His suits were invariably crisp,
his shirts buttoned at the neck
and his neckties smartly knotted.
No hair was ever out of place
and his nails were always pink and neatly trimmed.

He abhored loud noises,
a dropped spoon on a plate,
the kids or wife
shouting from another room,
rifle fire, muddy boots and rice.
He never watched movies about war,

lost dogs, lame horses,
or the frail and old dying in hospital.
He ate right, exercised, drank only in moderation
and never bit off more than he could chew.

He avoided people who talked
about how it was going to be
and those who talked about
how it used to be.
He liked his life exactly as it was.

And about his work
they said
he made you look better
than you were in life.
He was an artist with the dead.

When they asked him
why he choked his wife
he described how she malevolently taunted him
knowing what deeply disturbed him.
Insidiously she insisted on driving the car
though the hood ornament was askew.
Stubbornly she refused to pull over and straighten it.
And so at the red light he saw his opportunity and took it.
Clearly she made him do it.
She knew what he was like.
It was self defense.

Coffee

You look familiar
like I've seen you
somewhere before
do you know Joey Fats
from Hoboken
New Jersey
over the bridge
Angie's uncle
from Miami
Vito's partner
from the Bronx
a made guy
who owned the coffee shop
on Arthur Avenue
across the market
well Joey's doing time
Angie got chewed up by a shark
and died of complications

you want a long or short expresso

me I'm nobody
I'm a family man
I got five kids and a wife
Vito
nobody's seen Vito
for a long time

you take sugar
no I mean in your coffee

My Favorite White Tail Tall Tale

Bruno and I enjoy hunting
mushrooms in the woods,
he sniffs out the truffles and
leaves the above-ground stuff to me.
We love the scent of the moist loam
the dappled sunlight the luscious hush
that envelops us in these woods.

And so, on the first day
of deer hunting season
before the sun comes up
you'll find me at the Roscoe diner.
It's the place in the Catskill Mountains
where the city boys gather
all dressed in camouflage
to look like trees and bushes
and talk about their
shiny new guns
and trade tall tales
about the one that
got away last year.

And it's here where
through the aroma of
fresh-brewed coffee
fried eggs, bacon and
buttered toast that I begin
unwinding my tall tale
about the mysterious
12 point pure white stag
that lives on Darby Ridge.
He's as tall as a plow horse

and if you can see him
you can smell his musk.
No one has ever gotten off
a clean shot at him until now,
he seems to vanish at the crack
of the trigger squeeze.
I guess that's why he's a 12 pointer,
but I just don't know how
that stag could stand a chance
against all this fine camouflage
and high-power scoped guns
you boys are all sporting.

Darby Ridge, well, Darby Ridge
is eighteen miles northeast of here
at the dead end of Route 52.
Well, I gotta go now boys
before the rooster crows
and wakes up the missus.

Bruno and I
calmly walk our woods
knowing where all the
shaky itchy trigger fingers
will be for the day.
It's a perfect day for mushrooms here
eighteen miles southwest
of Darby Ridge.

Harvest Time

There are things we know about each other
that never need explaining
ash that settles on the running brook
and feeds the morning glory root.

We keep secret places
we return to in the night
private dreams
like lint in a deep pocket
that grows familiar to the touch.

The brook water dances under the morning sun.
The morning glories spread wide open.

We rub the slumber from our eyes
and stretch into the new day
where we nurture and reap and harvest
every seed we ever sowed
to live at the limits of imagination
together.

Sunday Visits

Visits to Aunt Tillie
meant scrubbing up
dressing up
sitting up
straight in a t-back chair
in the somber room
that smelled of church and old lace
where I said please
may I and thank you
for the cookies and milk
and the dollar she put in my pocket
but above all things
never ever even thought
if I didn't want to burn in hell forever
along with my whole white trash family
of not placing my cold milk glass
on the pink and blue flowered saucer
and branding the polished mahogany
with my bare sweaty glass of milk

Once
I forgot
and explained
in my ten year old way
that I enjoyed my visits so
it was my way
of leaving myself behind
because I didn't want to go

I got an extra dollar that day
for being a clever little boy
Aunt Tillie said
years and years before the wake

The Secret

The keyhole and the child's eye
like the sun and the morning
a needle and thread
or the courage of the child
who puts his eye to the door
and sees the red apple snuggled
in the crook of the yellow banana
the pregnant pear the orange
the purple grapes moist with dew
that overflow the rim of the blue bowl
glimpse the pigeon that furiously paces
coos and blinks
outside the closed window
while mom and dad lie safe and sound
Sunday morning behind the keyhole.

I rummage through the house
like a cat burglar
searching for the family secret
you surely admit to
now after all these years
as you turn in your warm bed
clinging to what you found
wrapped in linen
in the hat box
at the back of the closet
that day.

Hamlet in the Afternoon

From the start
I sensed that something was amiss
imagine would you
conversing with a ghost

I knew better then
the silliness of ghosts
only in my dreams
was dad with me and mom
and I was only six

This Hamlet was surely mad
or playing mad for us
slaying his uncle
and his mother too
for doing what he had in mind to do
marrying mom now that dad was gone

I knew all this at six
sitting in the darkened theater
on Wednesday afternoon
quiet and well behaved
between mom and Uncle Bob

And now years later
after a small fortune
and hours on the couch
I know for sure
what I felt then
that Hamlet was a wannabe
mother fucking murderer
playing innocent for the audience

And what about Ophelia
well what about her
she's my wife now
and the mother of our children
and we never do Shakespeare in the afternoon

Loss of Innocence

The dormant stone
that lies in the fallow field
absorbs the summer sun.
The crystal stream
chases itself
down the mountain pass.

The house beams stretch
and creak and crack awake
as the sap moves
through the limbs
of the living oak
and you remember images
from your innocent
picture coloring book
where what you thought
and what you said
were what you did
and who you were
in the color purple.

And then you were told
to strike a pose
beside your masterpiece
of the purple magnolia
spreading its budding branches
in the December snow
beside the orange cow
for posterity.

Framed posterity
sits on the mantlepiece
as the snows begin to melt.

It's All Good

It is all good
there is no meaning to it
turning it over in your palm
one line intersects the other
until you lose the pattern on the wall
where you hit just before
you hit the street at night
for rent and milk
and what you can not do without
that kills you while you keep alive

They warned you told you
mama and the welfare and the landlord
that love had nothing to do with it
while you believed the man
Simon could be reasoned with
Simon and Simon's daddy
were told what you were told
before your mama ever knew
Simon knows what side
his bread is buttered on
as he follows the lines
left by your palm
where line crosses line
and disappears from sight

Dry innocent snow gathers and swirls
around the crumpled figure on the ground
the infant holds tight against a warm breast
getting straight to keep alive while dying
the shadow on the alley wall
holds out a brightly colored sack

of jewels and gold coins
to buy the milk to pay the rent
and even buy the whole damned building

Something mama never knew
Simon never cast a shadow
and it is all good
at the very end of time
where every line intersects every line
in the palm of your hand
where it's all good
and safe from harm

Zen and Aunt Ida's Alphabet Soup

Remember all the Zen lectures
about arriving at Nirvana
where your mind becomes empty
of all mundane thoughts
of the here and now and the what for
and you enter a higher level
of being and not being
to become one with the universe
of blank non-verbal existence
if you quietly follow
in the Zen master's
soft-grass imprints.

Well I never got close
I was always too much
filled with Aunt Ida's
alphabet vegetable soup
and if my boy hair fell right
to attract the cute girl
that sat cross-legged next to me.

Aunt Ida however
got there all on her own
without any mystical lecture
from some barefoot
shmuck in a robe.

She sits by the window
in silence
and stares
the river Hudson flows
I feed her soup

and wipe her chin
I squeeze her hand
she squeezes back
she turns and turns back
to the flowing river
today like yesterday until tomorrow.

Falling from Your Mind

In your dream the memory has no punctuation
it starts in the middle in small case letters
where yesterday was decided
where tomorrow is a wish
where today could be if you wake up in time
before the devil sits on the throne
calling the shots behind closed doors
chasing his tail all the while in the dark

you dig around in your dream like a dog for a bone
for what you once felt
vague in your dream
gray in your brain
miles from your heart
the passion you buried in the flesh
like there was no tomorrow
or yesterday to dream about

as you fell from the air
you forgot about breathing
till you caught up with yourself on the way down

just as a comma breaks in on the line
and the devil chases his tail all the way to hell
where everybody knows is the hot place to be
where Rome burns and Nero fiddles

you make decisions
a cat jumps over the moon
and you move in your dream like the cat and the fiddle
to dance the night through

the bone and the flesh
that is waiting for you
at the end of this line
somewhere in your dream

M.I.A.

Something's missing
something feels not here
something's on my mind
that remains wordless
like a mute parrot
without a picture to fall back on
a dream a memory
you could count on for a thousand words
or more right about now
trapped inside a dumb feeling
gray and white and ice blue
that holds me frozen about the throat
lean cold fingers
keep my head up and my heart in place
connections do not meet
I'm lost or too late to get there on time
so I ride the line from end to end
reading my palm and the back of my hand
for a clue to where I might be
along the way
I pass a field of blue snowbells
crocuses and yellow daffs
yours for the having
as the ice melts and the ground thaws
and the brook runs babbling through the land
all yours for the having
if you look up
and out
the window

The Timeless Man

was not conscious of his beginning
as far as he knew
he always was
and since he had never
experienced his end
he assumed
he would always be
sitting by the running brook
where he became timeless
and his mind skipped over
the reflecting waters
that rushed by him
where life unfolded
in the moist mosses
along the still banks
as the brook careless of its beginning
clueless of its end
dependent only on its movement
reflects the golden autumn leaves.

The Man Who Went Too Far

In the cool October night
the gray weathered man
rows to the middle of the lake
and howls at the harvest moon

On the hilltop
the young gray wolves
howl at the same moon

And the wind howls unseen
through the pines

The gray man
looks up the hill
at the gray wolves
and listens in silence
to the howls and the invisible wind
that fill the spaces between the stars

Eagles gather in the morning mist
and circle 'round the still man

A solitary oar floats ashore

The lake
as always a calm reflection
holds the night secret from the prying day
the gray wolves
the gray man
the stars
the silence
are now invisible

The Man Who Waited
For the Sky to Fall

The man who waited
for the sky to fall
kept a peeled eye
on every apple
in his apple tree
from late summer
through early fall
determined
to spy the first ripe apple
that let go
and catch it
before it hit the ground.

He knew which trees were first and last
to shed their autumn leaves.
He always kept an eye on the sky.
He watched the birds fly south.
He watched the apples redden on the bough
and kept an eye out for early snow.

He knew someday the sky would fall.
The plump red apple relinquishes its grip.
The sky falls.
The apple hits the ground
as his slipper slides from his foot
and he slips into winter sleep
and the silent snow falls all around
the bright red apple on the ground.

Forget About It

Yesterday is as quiet
as new fallen snow.
Tomorrow is a word.
I pay close attention
to a fly on the golden apple.
I savor the sweet pungent
spice of my cigar.
I caress my feline companion
Mary Magdalene.
I eat what tastes good.
I watch the white clouds
behind the trees
until the darkness,
and then I watch the stars flicker.
I grow tired.
I sleep.
I dream of yesterday and tomorrow.
I smile,
but you can't see it in my dream.
I am happy.
Take my word for it.
I don't know about you,
but I've got it made.
So you can stop talking as if I weren't here.
And as for tomorrow,
well, sit with me and enjoy today.
It will be good for you
to forget for a while.

Do Over

Do nothing
sit there
do nothing
don't move
lift a finger
blink
swallow
think
or feel
just sit there and stare
there is nothing you can do
to change the unfolding story

Do nothing
you would not wish
done to you

Do nothing
do no harm
think yourself invisible

Walk with your bowed heads
into the ovens and showers

Sooner or later
we become our minds

Do unto others as
you would have them
do unto you

For Christ's sake
change your mind
change the story

Do something

What good
did thinking
ever do you

Do it for me

So What Took You So Long?

So what took you so long
is all I want to know
what were you doing
before you created this masterpiece
I admire your six-day focus
in doing what you did
and I get your need for a breather
after you got all that stuff done
and don't think I'm not grateful
for that free will thing
a blessing in disguise
if you get my drift
but what you were doing
before you got creative
you couldn't be thinking
because you always knew
what was what and what would be
so what were you doing
what took you so long
are you a dream
waiting to become a wish
we all dream of now and then
in the sleep of the night
we all postpone
for as long as it takes
for what you've had in mind
from the beginning
as day draws near
and the night is far on its course.

ABOUT THE AUTHOR

Marcus Rome is a psychoanalyst in private practice in New York City. *And This is What Happens Next* is his fourth book of poetry published by Birch Brook Press. His previous volumes are *Abreactions, Repercussions,* and *Confessions of a Rational Lunatic.*

ABOUT THE BOOK

And This is What Happens Next was set in 12 pt. Garamond on a Macintosh G4 by Pro-To-Type in Middletown, NY, and was printed and bound by Royal Fireworks Press, Unionville, NY. Birch Brook Press designed and published this book at Delhi, NY. Art by Bertha Rogers

Acknowledgments

These poems have appeared in the following publications:

"American Carminative," *Lilies and Cannonballs*, vol. 3 no. 2, 2008
"A Trace of Doubt," *Pacific Coast Journal*, vol. VIII no. iii, Fall 2005
"Coffee," *Laughing Dog*, issue no. 15, Fall/Winter 2007
"Hamlet in the Afternoon," *Mobius*, vol. XXIV, 2009
"Harvest Time," *Hidden Oak*, Fall 2005
"It's All Good," *Fluent Ascension*, issue 03.01, March 2006 (online)
    Straylight, Premier Issue, Spring 2007
"Loss of Innocence," *Mobius*, vol. XXIV, 2009
"Sunday Visits," *Rockford Review*, vol. XXVII no. 1, Winter/Spring '08
"The Last Word," *Fluent Ascension*, issue 03.01, March 2006 (online)
"The Timeless Man," *Hidden Oak*, Fall 2005

Forthcoming periodical publication of poems in this book:

"Falling from Your Mind," "Forget About It," "Safe House":
  Drama Garden
"So What Took You So Long?":
  Pyramid Arts & Poetry